2016 SQA Past Papers & Hodder Gibson Model Papers With Answers

National 5
DESIGN AND MANUFACTURE

Model Paper, 2014, 2015 & 2016 Exams

HODDER GIBSON
AN HACHETTE UK COMPANY

(spine) National 5 DESIGN AND MANUFACTURE

This book contains the official SQA 2014, 2015 and 2016 Exams for National 5 Design and Manufacture, with associated SQA-approved answers modified from the official marking instructions that accompany the paper.

In addition the book contains a model paper, together with answers, plus study skills advice. This paper, which may include a limited number of previously published SQA questions, has been specially commissioned by Hodder Gibson, and has been written by experienced senior teachers and examiners in line with the new National 5 syllabus and assessment outlines. This is not SQA material but has been devised to provide further practice for National 5 examinations.

Hodder Gibson is grateful to the copyright holders, as credited on the final page of the Answer Section, for permission to use their material. Every effort has been made to trace the copyright holders and to obtain their permission for the use of copyright material. Hodder Gibson will be happy to receive information allowing us to rectify any error or omission in future editions.

Hachette UK's policy is to use papers that are natural, renewable and recyclable products and made from wood grown in sustainable forests. The logging and manufacturing processes are expected to conform to the environmental regulations of the country of origin.

Orders: please contact Bookpoint Ltd, 130 Park Drive, Milton Park, Abingdon, Oxon OX14 4SE. Telephone: (44) 01235 827720. Fax: (44) 01235 400454. Lines are open 9.00–5.00, Monday to Saturday, with a 24-hour message answering service. Visit our website at www.hoddereducation.co.uk. Hodder Gibson can be contacted direct on: Tel: 0141 333 4650; Fax: 0141 404 8188; email: hoddergibson@hodder.co.uk

This collection first published in 2016 by
Hodder Gibson, an imprint of Hodder Education,
An Hachette UK Company
211 St Vincent Street
Glasgow G2 5QY

Typeset by Aptara, Inc.

Printed in the UK

A catalogue record for this title is available from the British Library

ISBN: 978-1-4718-9106-9

3 2 1

2017 2016

Introduction

Study Skills – what you need to know to pass exams!

Pause for thought

Many students might skip quickly through a page like this. After all, we all know how to revise. Do you really though?

Think about this:

"IF YOU ALWAYS DO WHAT YOU ALWAYS DO, YOU WILL ALWAYS GET WHAT YOU HAVE ALWAYS GOT."

Do you like the grades you get? Do you want to do better? If you get full marks in your assessment, then that's great! Change nothing! This section is just to help you get that little bit better than you already are.

There are two main parts to the advice on offer here. The first part highlights fairly obvious things but which are also very important. The second part makes suggestions about revision that you might not have thought about but which WILL help you.

Part 1

DOH! It's so obvious but …

Start revising in good time

Don't leave it until the last minute – this will make you panic.

Make a revision timetable that sets out work time AND play time.

Sleep and eat!

Obvious really, and very helpful. Avoid arguments or stressful things too – even games that wind you up. You need to be fit, awake and focused!

Know your place!

Make sure you know exactly **WHEN and WHERE** your exams are.

Know your enemy!

Make sure you know what to expect in the exam.

How is the paper structured?

How much time is there for each question?

What types of question are involved?

Which topics seem to come up time and time again?

Which topics are your strongest and which are your weakest?

Are all topics compulsory or are there choices?

Learn by DOING!

There is no substitute for past papers and practice papers – they are simply essential! Tackling this collection of papers and answers is exactly the right thing to be doing as your exams approach.

Part 2

People learn in different ways. Some like low light, some bright. Some like early morning, some like evening / night. Some prefer warm, some prefer cold. But everyone uses their BRAIN and the brain works when it is active. Passive learning – sitting gazing at notes – is the most INEFFICIENT way to learn anything. Below you will find tips and ideas for making your revision more effective and maybe even more enjoyable. What follows gets your brain active, and active learning works!

Activity 1 – Stop and review

Step 1

When you have done no more than 5 minutes of revision reading STOP!

Step 2

Write a heading in your own words which sums up the topic you have been revising.

Step 3

Write a summary of what you have revised in no more than two sentences. Don't fool yourself by saying, "I know it, but I cannot put it into words". That just means you don't know it well enough. If you cannot write your summary, revise that section again, knowing that you must write a summary at the end of it. Many of you will have notebooks full of blue/black ink writing. Many of the pages will not be especially attractive or memorable so try to liven them up a bit with colour as you are reviewing and rewriting. **This is a great memory aid, and memory is the most important thing.**

Activity 2 – Use technology!

Why should everything be written down? Have you thought about "mental" maps, diagrams, cartoons and colour to help you learn? And rather than write down notes, why not record your revision material?

What about having a text message revision session with friends? Keep in touch with them to find out how and what they are revising and share ideas and questions.

Why not make a video diary where you tell the camera what you are doing, what you think you have learned and what you still have to do? No one has to see or hear it, but the process of having to organise your thoughts in a formal way to explain something is a very important learning practice.

Be sure to make use of electronic files. You could begin to summarise your class notes. Your typing might be slow, but it will get faster and the typed notes will be easier to read than the scribbles in your class notes. Try to add different fonts and colours to make your work stand out. You can easily Google relevant pictures, cartoons and diagrams which you can copy and paste to make your work more attractive and **MEMORABLE**.

Activity 3 – This is it. Do this and you will know lots!

Step 1

In this task you must be very honest with yourself! Find the SQA syllabus for your subject (www.sqa.org.uk). Look at how it is broken down into main topics called MANDATORY knowledge. That means stuff you MUST know.

Step 2

BEFORE you do ANY revision on this topic, write a list of everything that you already know about the subject. It might be quite a long list but you only need to write it once. It shows you all the information that is already in your long-term memory so you know what parts you do not need to revise!

Step 3

Pick a chapter or section from your book or revision notes. Choose a fairly large section or a whole chapter to get the most out of this activity.

With a buddy, use Skype, Facetime, Twitter or any other communication you have, to play the game "If this is the answer, what is the question?". For example, if you are revising Geography and the answer you provide is "meander", your buddy would have to make up a question like "What is the word that describes a feature of a river where it flows slowly and bends often from side to side?".

Make up 10 "answers" based on the content of the chapter or section you are using. Give this to your buddy to solve while you solve theirs.

Step 4

Construct a wordsearch of at least 10 × 10 squares. You can make it as big as you like but keep it realistic. Work together with a group of friends. Many apps allow you to make wordsearch puzzles online. The words and phrases can go in any direction and phrases can be split. Your puzzle must only contain facts linked to the topic you are revising. Your task is to find 10 bits of information to hide in your puzzle, but you must not repeat information that you used in Step 3. DO NOT show where the words are. Fill up empty squares with random letters. Remember to keep a note of where your answers are hidden but do not show your friends. When you have a complete puzzle, exchange it with a friend to solve each other's puzzle.

Step 5

Now make up 10 questions (not "answers" this time) based on the same chapter used in the previous two tasks. Again, you must find NEW information that you have not yet used. Now it's getting hard to find that new information! Again, give your questions to a friend to answer.

Step 6

As you have been doing the puzzles, your brain has been actively searching for new information. Now write a NEW LIST that contains only the new information you have discovered when doing the puzzles. Your new list is the one to look at repeatedly for short bursts over the next few days. Try to remember more and more of it without looking at it. After a few days, you should be able to add words from your second list to your first list as you increase the information in your long-term memory.

FINALLY! Be inspired...

Make a list of different revision ideas and beside each one write **THINGS I HAVE** tried, **THINGS I WILL** try and **THINGS I MIGHT** try. Don't be scared of trying something new.

And remember – "FAIL TO PREPARE AND PREPARE TO FAIL!"

National 5 Design and Manufacture

The exam

The following guidance will give you a clear plan to take into the examination room and help you achieve better grades. The Design and Manufacture examination is split into two sections.

Section 1

Section 1 is worth 24 marks and will ask questions based around the workshop manufacturing techniques that could be used to manufacture a simple product. All the questions in this section will be about the product and its component parts. It is likely that there will be a mixture of materials used in the manufacture of the product. Those materials will most likely be wood, metal and plastic.

A good examination preparation strategy would be to ensure you have knowledge of the properties of a range of softwoods, hardwoods, ferrous and non-ferrous metals, thermoplastics and thermosetting plastics.

In addition, you will need to be familiar with common workshop processes using these materials. The tools and equipment used with these materials are also areas which you should study. Remember – none of this is new to you and you will have spent time on the Design and Manufacture course making a range of projects from these materials. Be confident.

Section 2

Section 2 is worth 36 marks and will ask questions mainly about the design part of the course, though there will be around 6 marks worth of manufacturing questions, which will ask about manufacturing in industry.

The design questions will come from a range of topics which you will have covered in the course, such as the design team, the design process, design factors, sketching, modelling, product evaluation and specifications.

A simple word can be used to help you remember the design factors: **FEEDSCAMP**

Each letter stands for one of the design factors: **F**unction, **E**rgonomics, **E**nvironmental concerns, **D**urability, **S**afety, **C**ost (economics), **A**esthetics, **M**aterials and **P**roduction.

If you use this as a memory aid, you should be able to answer any question that asks about design factors. There are obviously additional areas contained within these headings, but it is a great help to have one word that reminds you of all the areas.

For the rest of the questions in this section, you should think back through your course and the work you did in the Design Unit. This should help you answer the questions about the design process, sketching, modelling, specifications and the product evaluation activities you were involved with.

Where marks are commonly lost

One of the major problems that markers find is the lack of description in students' answers. When asked about design factors in relation to a given product, such as a kettle, the usual response is:

"The kettle should be safe and durable."

Although this is correct, we could be talking about any product on the planet, for example a watch should also be safe and durable.

To gain full marks, you should make clear reference to the product being asked about, so if we answer again about the kettle, the answer should be:

"It needs to be safe because the body of the kettle could get very hot with the boiling water and you could burn yourself. It needs to be durable because during the lifespan of a kettle it may get banged in the kitchen sink when being filled and it should withstand these collisions."

When you look at the response above you can clearly see that we are talking about a kettle now and not a watch. Try to do this through the whole of the paper, specifically in Section 2 when each question is about a different product.

Another area where candidates answer poorly is within the product evaluation question. You should try to extend your answers to fully describe the activities you would carry out with reference to the product being asked about. Too often responses are simplistic, for example, when being asked about evaluating the ease of use of a vacuum cleaner:

"They should do a user trial."

Or when being asked about value for money of a vacuum cleaner:

"They should do a comparison with other products."

Once again, these answers are correct, but do not explain the activity in any detail and would therefore not attract full marks.

An exemplar answer would be:

"They should carry out a user trial, where a range of users vacuum an area of carpet and then describe how easy or difficult they found the vacuum cleaner to manoeuvre around small items of furniture."

They should look at a range of existing vacuum cleaners that perform similar functions and see what their selling price is. They could then compare the selling price to theirs and this will show if their vacuum cleaner is good value for money."

Where improvements could be made to achieve better grades

If you want to achieve a better grade you should think about the way you answer other questions, such as questions that ask for "properties of materials that make them suitable for a particular product."

If you try to explain the properties of HDPE it may be difficult and the ones you choose may not relate directly to the product being asked about. Try to list the properties the product needs to have to be successful at its function. If we take the example of a milk container made from HDPE, we can then say that HDPE can be recycled, it is available in a range of colours and it is non-toxic. These are all "things" that the milk container does because it is a milk container not because it is made of HDPE. All of your properties of materials questions can be answered this way if you refer to "what the product needs to do" rather than the material.

The ergonomics question is where you could rack up vital extra marks. This question can be answered in lots of ways, but it is a good idea to have a plan before you go into the exam in case the ergonomics question is in the paper.

Think about the three aspects of ergonomics: anthropometrics, physiology and psychology.

Try to write two answers for each area relating to the product in the question.

There is a simple formula to help you get full marks in this question.

For anthropometrics, pick a part of the product and then pick a part of the human body that should fit on/into that part. Link them together in a sentence and you get one mark. Do that twice to get full marks. E.g. Kettle: the handle of the kettle should fit the adult male palm width.

For physiology, pick a part of the product and then come up with a verb that you would do with that part. Link them together in a sentence and you get one mark. Do that twice to get full marks. E.g. Kettle: filling should be easy so the lid should be easy to open.

For psychology, pick a part of the product and then come up with a feeling or emotion to do with that part. Link them together in a sentence and you get one mark. Do that twice to get full marks. E.g. Kettle: the switch on the kettle should make a clicking sound to let you know that it is on.

Good luck!

Remember that the rewards for passing National 5 Design and Manufacture are well worth it! Your pass will help you get the future you want for yourself. In the exam, be confident in your own ability. If you're not sure how to answer a question trust your instincts and just give it a go anyway. Keep calm and don't panic! GOOD LUCK!

NATIONAL 5

Model Paper

Whilst this Model Paper has been specially commissioned by Hodder Gibson for use as practice for the National 5 exams, the key reference documents remain the SQA Specimen Paper 2013 and the SQA Past Papers 2014, 2015 and 2016.

National
Qualifications
MODEL PAPER

Design and Manufacture

Duration — 1 hour and 30 minutes

Total marks — 60

SECTION 1 — 24 marks

Attempt ALL questions.

SECTION 2 — 36 marks

Attempt ALL questions.

Read every question carefully before you attempt it.

Write your answers clearly in the spaces provided, using **blue** or **black** ink.

Show all working and units where appropriate.

Before leaving the examination room you must give this booklet to the Invigilator.
If you do not, you may lose all the marks for this paper.

SECTION 1 — 24 marks

Attempt ALL questions

1. A small storage container is shown below.

(a) The container was manufactured mainly from softwood.

State the name of **two** suitable softwoods that could have been used.   2

_____

_____

(b) The back of the container is made from plywood as shown below.

1. (b) (continued)

    (i) Describe the benefits of using plywood for the back of the container.   **2**

    (ii) State the name of **two** other manufactured boards that could have been used.   **2**

(c) The drawer of the container is shown below.

    (i) State the name of **two** suitable joining techniques that could have been used at each corner of the drawer.   **2**

    (ii) Describe, with reference to tools, the way that one of the joints you have named above could be manufactured in the workshop using hand tools.   **3**

The drawer has a 20mm diameter hole for opening instead of a handle.

    (iii) Describe, with reference to tools and machinery, the way that the 20mm hole could have been manufactured in the workshop.   **3**

1. (continued) **MARKS** DO NOT WRITE IN THIS MARGIN

The container has been finished with wax.

(d) Describe the benefits of using wax to finish the surfaces of the container. **2**

(e) The decorative plastic photo-frame shown below was added to the top of the container.

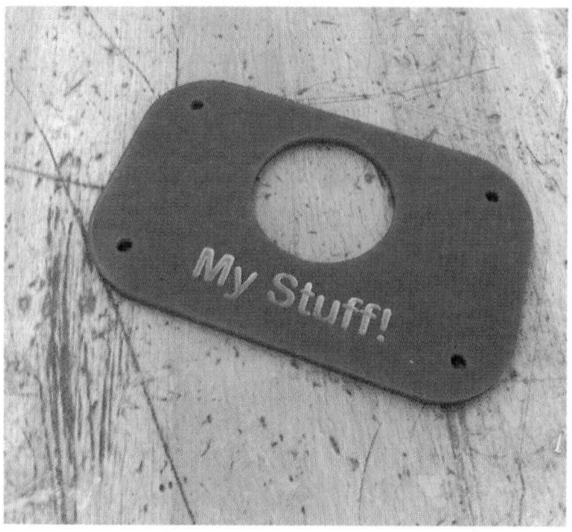

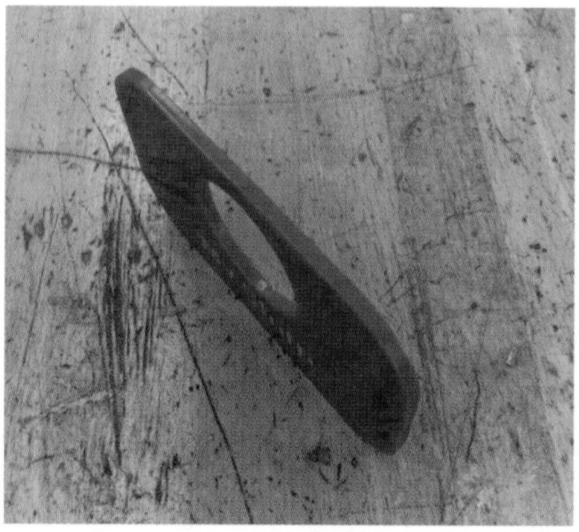

(i) Describe, with reference to tools, the way the four holes would have been marked out in the workshop. **3**

(ii) Describe the stages that would be carried out to make the edges of the plastic smooth and shiny. **4**

The screws and eyelets used to join the plastic to the container were manufactured from a non-ferrous metal

(iii) State the name of a suitable non-ferrous metal. **1**

Total marks 24

SECTION 2 — 36 marks

Attempt ALL questions

MARKS | DO NOT WRITE IN THIS MARGIN

2. Computer mice are shown below.

Before producing a specification for a computer mouse the designer would have researched various design issues.

With reference to a computer mouse, state **four** design issues which would have been researched and explain why each of these design issues is important.

5

_____

_____

_____

_____

_____

_____

_____

_____

_____

_____

_____

_____

_____

3. A child's activity toy is shown below.

Describe how the design of the activity toy has been influenced by ergonomics.   6

_____

_____

_____

_____

_____

_____

_____

_____

_____

_____

_____

_____

_____

_____

_____

_____

4. During the design process, a designer will use various materials to build models.

    (a) State **two** reasons why the designer would build models.   2

    _____

    _____

4. (continued) MARKS | DO NOT WRITE IN THIS MARGIN

(b) State the name of **two** materials that could be used to produce models and explain why each material is suitable. **4**

(Note: a different explanation should be given for each material.)

____

____

____

____

Total marks 6

5. A portable gas camping stove is shown below.

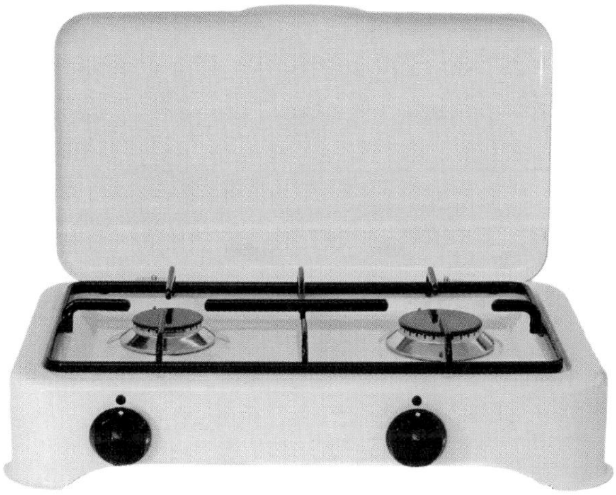

(a) Describe how each of the following issues has influenced the design of the camping stove.

(i) Environment **2**

____

____

(ii) Safety **2**

____

____

(b) The camping stove could be described as being attractive to a niche market. Explain the term **"niche market"**. **2**

____

____

____

Total marks 6

6. A pocket multi-tool manufactured from stainless steel is shown below.   **MARKS**

(a) With reference to the above multi-tool, describe the difference between primary and secondary functions.   **2**

_____

_____

(b) Describe a technique that could be used to evaluate the ease of use of the multi-tool.   **2**

_____

_____

(c) Describe the aesthetic qualities of the multi-tool.   **2**

_____

_____

(d) State **one** reason why the designer has chosen stainless steel for this product.   **1**

_____

_____

(e) State **two** methods of applying a coloured finish to the handles.   **2**

_____

_____

Total marks   9

7. The ability to generate ideas is an important aspect of a designer's work.

(a) State **two** idea generation techniques.

2

_____

_____

(b) Describe how one of these techniques would be carried out.

2

_____

_____

_____

_____

Total marks   4

[END OF MODEL PAPER]

[BLANK PAGE]

DO NOT WRITE ON THIS PAGE

NATIONAL 5

2014

N5

National Qualifications 2014

Mark

X719/75/01

Design and Manufacture

TUESDAY, 27 MAY
1:00 PM – 2:30 PM

Fill in these boxes and read what is printed below.

Full name of centre

Town

Forename(s)

Surname

Number of seat

Date of birth

Day	Month	Year
D D	M M	Y Y

Scottish candidate number

Total marks — 60

SECTION 1 — 24 marks

Attempt ALL questions.

SECTION 2 — 36 marks

Attempt ALL questions.

Write your answers clearly in the spaces provided in this booklet. Additional space for answers is provided at the end of this booklet. If you use this space you must clearly identify the question number you are attempting.

Use **blue** or **black** ink.

Before leaving the examination room you must give this booklet to the Invigilator; if you do not, you may lose all the marks for this paper.

MARKS | DO NOT WRITE IN THIS MARGIN

SECTION 1 — 24 marks
Attempt ALL questions

1. A chess box is shown below.

(a) Hardwood was used for some of the squares of the chess board.

   (i) State the name of a hardwood that could have been used for the squares.   **1**

   _____

   (ii) Describe **two** benefits of using hardwoods for the manufacture of this product.   **2**

   _____

   _____

(b) A comb joint has been used at each corner.

   State the name of **two** alternative joints that could have been used at each corner.   **2**

   _____

   _____

(c) Clear varnish was used as a surface finish for the chess box.

   (i) Describe **two** benefits of using clear varnish as a surface finish for the chess box.   **2**

   _____

   _____

MARKS | DO NOT WRITE IN THIS MARGIN

1. (c) (continued)

(ii) Describe **two** stages in the preparation of the wood before applying the varnish.

2

_____

_____

The plastic tray shown below was vacuum formed and is used to hold the chess pieces. The wooden pattern used in the process is also shown.

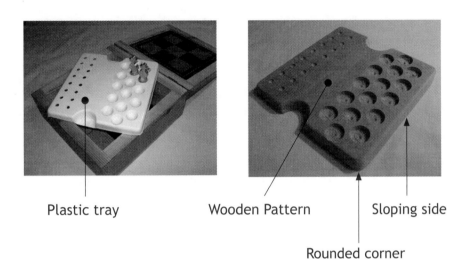

Plastic tray   Wooden Pattern   Sloping side

Rounded corner

(d) Explain the reason for the following features in the wooden pattern.

(i) Rounded corners _____   1

_____

(ii) Sloping sides _____   1

_____

(iii) A thermoplastic was used for the tray.

Describe **two** benefits of using a thermoplastic for this type of product.

2

_____

_____

_____

_____

[Turn over

MARKS | DO NOT WRITE IN THIS MARGIN

1. (continued)

(e) The aluminium handle shown below was manufactured using a centre lathe.

Chamfer ———— Parallel Turned Dowel

Describe how **each** of the following processes would be carried out on the centre lathe to manufacture the handle.

(i) Chamfering 2

_____

_____

_____

_____

(ii) Parallel turning 2

_____

_____

_____

_____

(iii) A change of speed may be required when using a centre lathe.

State **two** reasons why a change in lathe speed may be necessary. 2

_____

_____

_____

_____

_____

MARKS

1. (continued)

(f) The aluminium chess pieces shown below were commercially produced by the process of die casting.

(i) State **two** reasons for using aluminium for the chess pieces.   2

_____

_____

_____

_____

(ii) State **three** benefits of using die casting to manufacture the chess pieces.   3

_____

_____

_____

_____

_____

_____

Total marks   24

[Turn over

MARKS | DO NOT WRITE IN THIS MARGIN

SECTION 2 — 36 marks

Attempt ALL questions

2. The 2012 Olympic success of Team GB caused an increased interest in all forms of cycling for all ages.

(a) Describe how ergonomics has influenced the design of bicycles.

6

_____

_____

_____

_____

_____

_____

_____

_____

_____

_____

_____

_____

_____

MARKS

2. (continued)

(b) Before producing a design specification for a bicycle, the designer would have researched various design factors.

Explain why the following design factors would be researched when designing bicycles.

(i) Durability   1

_____

_____

_____

_____

(ii) Ease of maintenance   1

_____

_____

_____

_____

(iii) Aesthetics   1

_____

_____

_____

_____

Total marks   9

[Turn over

3. The environmental impact of a product can often influence our buying decisions.

Explain ways in which designers could reduce the environmental impact of their products.

(*You may wish to refer to products with which you are familiar.*)

3

MARKS

DO NOT
WRITE
IN THIS
MARGIN

4. Designers use a range of graphic techniques to communicate their designs.

(a) State the name of **one** graphic technique that the designer may use at each of the following stages of the design process **and** explain why it would be suitable.

(*A different graphic technique must be used for each stage.*)

  (i) Initial ideas

2

_____

_____

_____

_____

  (ii) Planning for manufacture

2

_____

_____

_____

_____

[Turn over

MARKS

4. (continued)

(b) Designers often use models as well as a range of graphic techniques.

State the name of **two** modelling materials and explain why each would be suitable for building models.

(*A different explanation must be given for each material.*)

4

_____

_____

_____

_____

_____

_____

_____

_____

Total marks   8

MARKS | DO NOT WRITE IN THIS MARGIN

5. A stainless steel colander is shown below.

(a) (i) Give **two** reasons why stainless steel would be suitable for the colander.

2

_____

_____

_____

_____

(ii) The colander was mass produced.

Describe **two** benefits to the manufacturer of mass production techniques.

2

_____

_____

_____

_____

[Turn over

MARKS | DO NOT WRITE IN THIS MARGIN

5. (continued)

(b) Colanders can also be manufactured from plastic as shown below.

State the name of a suitable process for manufacturing colanders from plastic.

1

_____

(c) Manufacturers are increasingly using CNC and CADCAM technologies to make their products.

Describe the impact that these technologies have on the manufacturer.

3

_____

_____

_____

_____

_____

_____

_____

_____

_____

_____

_____

Total marks   8

MARKS

6. An electric razor is shown below.

The manufacturer wishes to carry out an evaluation of the razor.

(a) Describe a suitable user trial to evaluate the ergonomics of the razor.　　2

_____

_____

_____

_____

(b) State **two** key questions that would be included in a survey to evaluate the aesthetics of the razor.　　2

_____

_____

_____

_____

[Turn over for Question 6 (c) on *Page fourteen*

MARKS | DO NOT WRITE IN THIS MARGIN

6. (continued)

(c) There are a wide variety of razors available on the market today.

With such a large selection, designers need to find ways of marketing their product in order to make it stand out from the competition.

Describe **two** marketing techniques that a design team may use to promote their product.

2

_____

_____

_____

_____

_____

_____

(d) Designers often have to generate new ideas to stay ahead of their competitors.

Describe **one** idea generation technique that they could use.

2

_____

_____

_____

_____

_____

_____

Total marks   8

[END OF QUESTION PAPER]

MARKS

DO NOT
WRITE
IN THIS
MARGIN

ADDITIONAL SPACE FOR ANSWERS

MARKS

DO NOT WRITE IN THIS MARGIN

ADDITIONAL SPACE FOR ANSWERS

NATIONAL 5

2015

N5

National Qualifications 2015

Mark

X719/75/01

Design and Manufacture

MONDAY, 25 MAY

1:00 PM – 2:30 PM

Fill in these boxes and read what is printed below.

Full name of centre

Town

Forename(s)

Surname

Number of seat

Date of birth

| Day | Month | Year | Scottish candidate number |

Total marks — 60

SECTION 1 — 24 marks

Attempt ALL questions.

SECTION 2 — 36 marks

Attempt ALL questions.

Write your answers clearly in the spaces provided in this booklet. Additional space for answers is provided at the end of this booklet. If you use this space you must clearly identify the question number you are attempting.

Use **blue** or **black** ink.

Before leaving the examination room you must give this booklet to the Invigilator; if you do not, you may lose all the marks for this paper.

MARKS | DO NOT WRITE IN THIS MARGIN

SECTION 1 — 24 MARKS

Attempt ALL questions

1. A design for a toy helicopter is shown below.

(a) The main body of the helicopter was manufactured by laminating two pieces of hardwood and one piece of softwood.

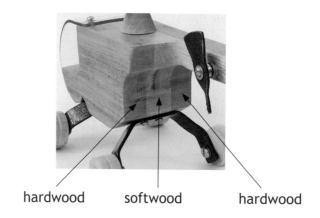

hardwood   softwood   hardwood

MARKS | DO NOT WRITE IN THIS MARGIN

1. (a) (continued)

(i) The pieces of wood were glued together to form a strong, permanent join.

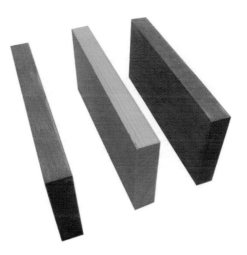

State **one** suitable piece of equipment that could have been used to hold the wood securely, during the drying of the glue.

1

_____

_____

(ii) Describe **two** environmental considerations when selecting hardwood for the main body of the helicopter.

2

_____

_____

_____

_____

[Turn over

MARKS | DO NOT WRITE IN THIS MARGIN

1. **(continued)**

(b) The legs on the underside of the helicopter are made from mild steel.

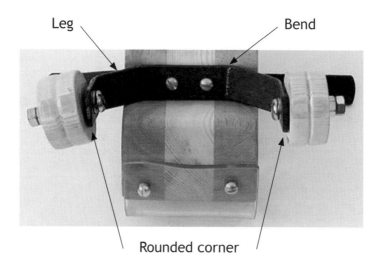

Leg   Bend

Rounded corner

The legs were drilled and rounded before bending as shown below.

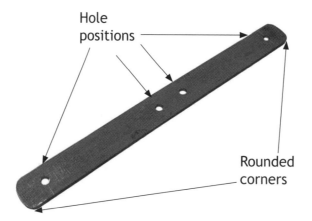

Hole positions

Rounded corners

(i) Describe, with reference to appropriate tools, **two** stages in marking out the positions of the holes on the legs as shown above.   2

_____

_____

_____

_____

MARKS | DO NOT WRITE IN THIS MARGIN

1. (b) (continued)

(ii) Describe **two** stages required to shape the rounded corners on the legs.

2

_____

_____

_____

_____

(iii) Describe **two** stages required to form the bends in the legs.

Bends in legs

2

_____

_____

_____

(iv) Describe how multiple sets of legs could be manufactured to be identical if the helicopter was batch produced.

1

_____

_____

_____

_____

[Turn over

MARKS | DO NOT WRITE IN THIS MARGIN

1. (b) (continued)

(v) Gloss paint was chosen as a suitable finish for the legs.

Describe **two** stages in the preparation of the metal before applying the paint.

2

_____

_____

_____

_____

MARKS | DO NOT WRITE IN THIS MARGIN

1. (continued)

(c) The windscreen of the helicopter is manufactured from acrylic sheet.

(i) State **two** properties of acrylic sheet that make it a suitable choice of material for the windscreen.

2

_____

_____

_____

(ii) After drilling, the windscreen was formed into a curve.

Curve ——→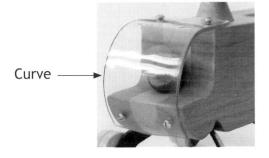

Describe **two** stages carried out during the process of forming the curve.

2

_____

_____

_____

_____

MARKS | DO NOT WRITE IN THIS MARGIN

1. (continued)

(d) The wooden wheels were turned on a woodturning lathe from a single piece of softwood.

(i) Describe **three** stages in preparing the softwood blank **before** fitting it on the woodturning lathe. Sketches may be used to illustrate your answer.

3

_____

_____

_____

_____

_____

_____

_____

MARKS | DO NOT WRITE IN THIS MARGIN

1. (d) (continued)

(ii) Describe **two** stages that could be carried out on the woodturning lathe to improve the surface finish on the four wheels.

Wheels

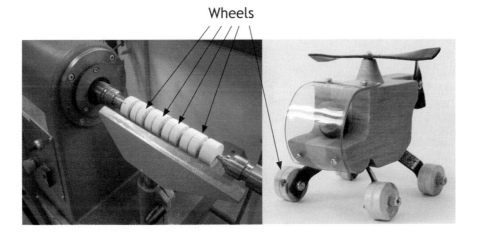

2

_____

_____

_____

_____

(e) The target market for the helicopter is young children.

Describe **two** ways in which the helicopter could be made more appealing to the target market.

2

_____

_____

_____

_____

(f) The helicopter has been designed to have a long lifespan.

State **one** benefit to the environment of this design decision.

1

_____

_____

_____

MARKS | DO NOT WRITE IN THIS MARGIN

SECTION 2 — 36 marks

Attempt ALL questions

2. Creative use of modern materials and manufacturing methods has made products like this clock easier to produce.

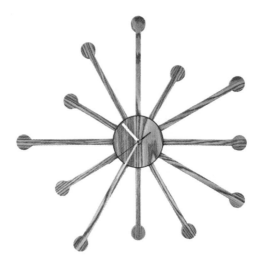

(a) The plywood components of the clock were manufactured using Computer Aided Manufacture (CAM).

   (i) State **one** benefit to the manufacturer of using plywood for the clock.

   1

   _____

   _____

   (ii) State the name of **one** suitable CAM method for cutting the plywood components of the clock.

   1

   _____

   (iii) Describe **two** benefits to the manufacturer of using CAM.

   2

   _____

   _____

   _____

   _____

MARKS | DO NOT WRITE IN THIS MARGIN

2. (continued)

(b) The clock is sold as a self-assembly kit.

Explain **two** quality assurance issues relating to self-assembly kits.   2

_____

_____

_____

_____

_____

_____

[Turn over

MARKS | DO NOT WRITE IN THIS MARGIN

3.   When designing hand held products similar to the dish brush shown below, the designer will use a range of techniques to reach the final design proposal.

(a)   Idea generation techniques were used during the design of the dish brush.

(i)   State the name of **two** idea generation techniques.   2

_____

_____

(ii)   Describe how **one** of your stated idea generation techniques would be carried out.   2

(Sketches may be used to illustrate your answer).

_____

_____

_____

_____

MARKS | DO NOT WRITE IN THIS MARGIN

3. (continued)

(b) To communicate the designs, a range of graphic techniques were used.

State the name of **one** graphic technique that the designer may use at each of the following stages of the design process **and** explain why it would be suitable.

(*a different graphic technique must be used for each stage.*)

(i)   Development of ideas   2

_____

_____

_____

(ii) Communicating design proposal to client   2

_____

_____

_____

(c) Various models of the dish brush were produced.

(i)   State **two** reasons why the designer would use models when designing the dish brush.   2

_____

_____

_____

(ii) State the name of a suitable modelling material that could be used to make a model of the dish brush handle.   1

_____

[Turn over

MARKS | DO NOT WRITE IN THIS MARGIN

4. Aesthetics is an important factor in the design of the wireless headphones shown below.

Headphones A   Headphones B

Headphones C

(a) Describe the aesthetic qualities of the headphones.   3

[*You may wish to refer to one, two or all of the headphones shown above*]

_____

_____

_____

_____

_____

_____

MARKS | DO NOT WRITE IN THIS MARGIN

4. (continued)

(b) Anthropometrics is important in the design of headphones.

Describe **two** ways in which the design of headphones has been influenced by anthropometrics.

2

_____

_____

_____

_____

_____

(c) State **two** functional benefits of wireless headphones.

2

_____

_____

_____

_____

[Turn over

MARKS | DO NOT WRITE IN THIS MARGIN

5. A design team is developing a new scooter similar to the one shown below.

The market researcher in the design team plans to carry out a product evaluation.

(a) Describe a suitable test to evaluate the durability of the scooter.

2

_____

_____

_____

_____

(b) Describe a suitable evaluation technique to find out if the scooter would be good value for money.

2

_____

_____

_____

_____

MARKS | DO NOT WRITE IN THIS MARGIN

5.   (continued)

(c)   A design specification is required for the scooter.

Write **one** specification statement for each of the following:

(i)   Function   1

_____

_____

_____

(ii)   Ease of maintenance   1

_____

_____

_____

(d)   There are a number of members in a design team.

Describe the role of:

(i)   The Engineer   1

_____

_____

_____

(ii)   The Accountant   1

_____

_____

_____

[Turn over for Question 6 on *Page eighteen*

MARKS | DO NOT WRITE IN THIS MARGIN

6.   Injection moulded plastic building blocks are shown below.

(a) State **two** initial set-up costs of injection moulding.   2

_____

_____

(b) State **two** visual features that indicate a product has been injection moulded.   2

_____

_____

[END OF QUESTION PAPER]

MARKS | DO NOT WRITE IN THIS MARGIN

ADDITIONAL SPACE FOR ANSWERS

MARKS | DO NOT WRITE IN THIS MARGIN

ADDITIONAL SPACE FOR ANSWERS

NATIONAL 5

2016

N5

National Qualifications 2016

Mark

X719/75/01

Design and Manufacture

THURSDAY, 2 JUNE
9:00 AM — 10:30 AM

Fill in these boxes and read what is printed below.

Full name of centre

Town

Forename(s)

Surname

Number of seat

Date of birth

Day	Month	Year	Scottish candidate number

Total marks — 60

SECTION 1 — 24 marks

Attempt ALL questions.

SECTION 2 — 36 marks

Attempt ALL questions.

Write your answers clearly in the spaces provided in this booklet. Additional space for answers is provided at the end of this booklet. If you use this space you must clearly identify the question number you are attempting.

Use **blue** or **black** ink.

Before leaving the examination room you must give this booklet to the Invigilator; if you do not, you may lose all the marks for this paper.

SQA

SECTION 1 — 24 MARKS
Attempt ALL questions

1. A pupil's project for a combined spinner and wind chime is shown below.

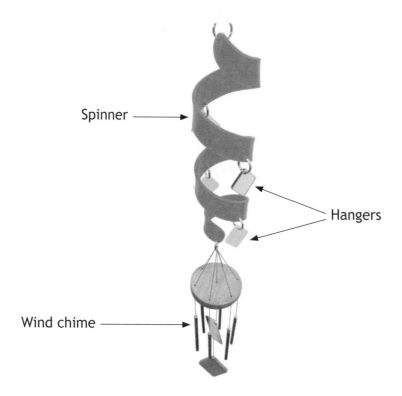

Spinner

Hangers

Wind chime

(a) The spinner was manufactured from a strip of low cost sheet thermoplastic as shown below.

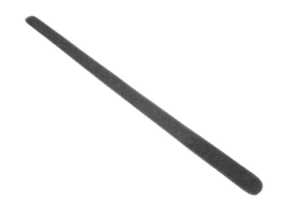

(i) State **two** reasons (other than low cost) why thermoplastic is a suitable material for the spinner.

2

_____

_____

MARKS | DO NOT WRITE IN THIS MARGIN

1. (a) (continued)

(ii) The strip of thermoplastic was formed into the shape shown below.

Describe how the twists in the thermoplastic strip could be formed.   2

_____

_____

_____

_____

_____

_____

[Turn over

MARKS | DO NOT WRITE IN THIS MARGIN

1. (a) (continued)

The edges were finished before forming the strip.

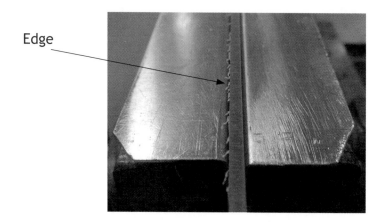

Edge

(iii) State **two** reasons why finishing before forming was suitable.   2

_____

_____

_____

_____

(b) The thermoplastic hangers were marked out and then clamped in an engineer's vice using aluminium soft jaws.

Waste material between square hangers   Aluminium soft jaw

(i) Explain why waste material was left between the two marked out squares.   1

_____

_____

MARKS | DO NOT WRITE IN THIS MARGIN

1. (b) (continued)

   (ii) Explain why aluminium soft jaws were used to clamp the piece of thermoplastic.   1

   _____

   _____

(c) Beech was selected for the top of the wind chime.

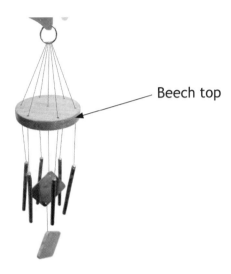

Beech top

State **two** reasons why beech was suitable for the top of the wind chime.   2

   _____

   _____

   _____

   _____

(d) The beech was sourced from a sustainable forest.

   Explain the term *"sustainable forest"*.   1

   _____

   _____

[Turn over

MARKS | DO NOT WRITE IN THIS MARGIN

1. (continued)

(e) A hole was drilled in the centre of the piece of beech as shown below.

(i) Describe how the position of the central hole could be marked out accurately making reference to workshop tools.

(You may sketch on the graphic to show your answer.)

2

_____

_____

_____

_____

(ii) Varnish was applied to the beech top.

State **two** benefits of using varnish for the beech top.

2

_____

_____

MARKS | DO NOT WRITE IN THIS MARGIN

1. (e) (continued)

(iii) Describe how the beech top could be finished to a high standard.   3

(*You must refer to applying the finish and surface preparation stages to gain full marks.*)

_____

_____

_____

_____

_____

_____

_____

_____

[Turn over

MARKS | DO NOT WRITE IN THIS MARGIN

1.   (continued)

(f)   The chimes were made from a length of 6 mm diameter brass bar.

State **two** reasons why brass was a suitable choice of material for the chimes.

2

_____

_____

_____

_____

MARKS

1. (continued)

(g) The chime shown below was manufactured from the length of 6 mm diameter brass bar.

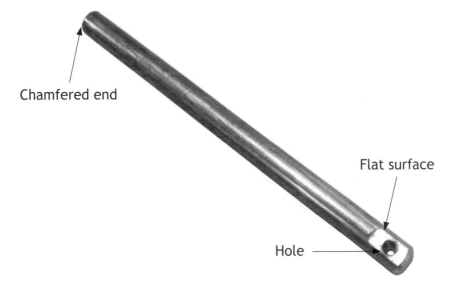

Chamfered end

Flat surface

Hole

Describe how the chime would be manufactured with reference to workshop tools.

4

_____

_____

_____

_____

_____

_____

_____

_____

_____

_____

_____

_____

MARKS | DO NOT WRITE IN THIS MARGIN

SECTION 2 — 36 MARKS
Attempt ALL questions

2. A washing machine is shown below.

The manufacturer wishes to carry out an evaluation of the washing machine.

(a) Describe a suitable test that could be carried out to evaluate the function of the washing machine.

2

_____

_____

_____

_____

(b) Describe **two** ways in which the designers could reduce the environmental impact of the washing machine.

2

_____

_____

_____

_____

MARKS | DO NOT WRITE IN THIS MARGIN

2.   (continued)

(c)   The metal hinge shown below was mass produced.

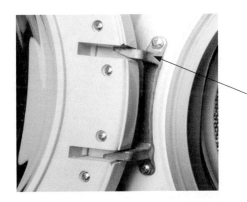

Metal hinge

(i)   State the name of a suitable process which would allow the hinge to be manufactured with minimal finishing.   **1**

_____

(ii)   State the name of a suitable material for the hinge.   **1**

_____

(iii)   Prior to final manufacturing, the hinge was rapid prototyped on a 3D printer.

Describe **two** benefits to the manufacturer of rapid prototyping the hinge.   **2**

_____

_____

_____

_____

[Turn over

MARKS | DO NOT WRITE IN THIS MARGIN

3. A "smart" wrist band used when exercising, is shown below.

(a) Describe the influence the following design factors have on this type of product.

    (i) Ergonomics   4

_____

_____

_____

_____

_____

_____

_____

_____

_____

_____

    (ii) Durability   2

_____

_____

_____

_____

MARKS | DO NOT WRITE IN THIS MARGIN

3. **(a)** **(continued)**

    (iii) Aesthetics   2

    _____

    _____

    _____

    _____

    _____

  (b) The design was created to satisfy a market niche and was influenced by market pull.

    (i) Explain the term "*market niche*".   1

    _____

    _____

    _____

    (ii) Explain the term "*market pull*".   1

    _____

    _____

    _____

  (c) The thermoplastic outer casing of the wrist band was manufactured by the process of injection moulding.

    State the name of a suitable thermoplastic that could have been used **and** describe why it is suitable.   2

    _____

    _____

    _____

    _____

                                          [Turn over

MARKS | DO NOT WRITE IN THIS MARGIN

4.   When designing cars the design team will use a range of models.

Dmitry Morgan / Shutterstock.com

(a)   State **two** benefits to the designer of using computer generated models.   **2**

_____

_____

_____

Standard components are often used in car production.

(b)   Describe **two** benefits to the manufacturer of using standard components.   **2**

_____

_____

_____

_____

_____

The cars will be produced using computer aided manufacturing (CAM) systems.

(c)   Describe **two** drawbacks to the manufacturer of using these systems.   **2**

_____

_____

_____

_____

_____

MARKS | DO NOT WRITE IN THIS MARGIN

4. **(continued)**

The cars were launched under a successful brand name.

(d) Describe **two** benefits of launching a product under a successful brand name.

2

_____

_____

_____

_____

[Turn over

MARKS | DO NOT WRITE IN THIS MARGIN

5. A mood board is shown below.

meunierd/Shutterstock.com

(a) Describe how a mood board could be used to generate ideas.   2

_____

_____

_____

_____

_____

(b) The following **open design brief** was given to the designer:

   "Design lighting inspired by the Art Deco design movement."

   State **two** benefits of an open design brief.   2

_____

_____

_____

_____

_____

MARKS | DO NOT WRITE IN THIS MARGIN

5.   (continued)

(c) Designers use a range of graphic techniques throughout the design process.

State the name of **one** graphic technique that the designer may use at each of the following stages of the design process **and** explain why it would be suitable.

(*A different graphic technique **and** explanation must be used for each stage.*)

(i)   Initial Ideas   2

_____

_____

_____

_____

_____

_____

(ii) Planning for manufacture   2

_____

_____

_____

_____

_____

_____

[END OF QUESTION PAPER]

MARKS | DO NOT WRITE IN THIS MARGIN

ADDITIONAL SPACE FOR ANSWERS

MARKS DO NOT WRITE IN THIS MARGIN

ADDITIONAL SPACE FOR ANSWERS

[BLANK PAGE]

DO NOT WRITE ON THIS PAGE

NATIONAL 5

Answers

NATIONAL 5 DESIGN AND MANUFACTURE MODEL PAPER

SECTION 1

1. (a) Pine, Spruce

   (b) (i) Plywood is strong in all directions and will not warp or bend after fitting.
       (ii) MDF, hardboard

   (c) (i) Lap joint, dovetail joint
       (ii) **Lap joint:** after marking out the joint with a try square, marking gauge and rule, you would cut down halfway through the wood with a tenon saw. Then you would chisel out the waste wood with a bevel edged chisel. Finally you could use a hand router to smooth the bottom of the lap joint.
       (iii) **20mm hole:** after marking out with a rule and a try square, you would fit a forstener bit to the pillar drill. You would then drill slowly through the wood to make sure you don't split it at the back.

   (d) Wax makes the container look good and it also makes it more durable and helps to protect the wood from rotting.

   (e) (i) The four holes would have been marked out by using a rule, scriber and engineers square: the rule would be used to measure along the edge of the acrylic to the desired size, this would be marked by the scriber. Then the engineers square would be used with the scriber to mark out the positions of the holes.
       (ii) There are four usual stages, these are cross file, draw file, wet and dry paper or block and finally applying polish with a cloth.
       (iii) Brass

SECTION 2

2. The designer would research: Function, ergonomics, durability and safety.
   - **Function:** The mouse will need to perform several operations such as scrolling and multi-button use.
   - **Ergonomics:** The mouse will need to be the right size for most users' hands.
   - **Durability:** The mouse will need to be able to withstand being used every day and not wear away.
   - **Safety:** The mouse has some electrical connection and therefore it will need to be safe for the user to hold it and not get an electric shock.

   One mark for the four issues, one mark for each explanation.

3. *Candidates have three possible routes to go down in their response: anthropometrics, physiology and psychology. There is no requirement to refer to any of these areas by name. Typical responses within each aspect are shown below. Six suitable responses will gain six marks. Any suitable answer relating human dimensions and relevant aspect of the activity toy should be awarded one mark, e.g. The slide width has been designed to suit child hip breadth.*

   Other suitable answers:
   - Width/length of treads — body/foot/leg width
   - Diameter of ladder frame — grip diameter
   - Vertical distance between treads — leg stretch
   - Height of handrail — arm reach/stretch

   Any suitable answer relating to human limitations, linking to part of the activity toy should be awarded one mark.

   The use of physical action verbs linking to the use of the activity toy are to be looked for here, e.g. the activity toy has been designed to be moved easily by an adult around the garden.

   Other suitable answers:
   - The activity toy — moving, lifting, dragging, shifting
   - Tread spacing — leg raise, climbing

   Any suitable answer relating to human thoughts/feelings/ emotions, linking to part or bit of the activity toy should be awarded one mark, e.g. the choice of bright/warm/ advancing coloured material on the slide will ensure that the user knows which part is the fun part.

   Other suitable answers:
   - Bumpy appearance — fun/exciting
   - Robust appearance — feeling of safety (for child/ parent/carer)/stability
   - Bright colours — fun

4. (a) • Models are used to develop an idea by giving a three dimensional view of a concept.
       • Models can be used to test for ergonomic and aesthetic decision making.

   One mark per correct response up to total of two marks.

   (b) Possible materials range from modelling clay through to wire, plywood, acrylic and smart modelling materials.

   One mark awarded for the correct naming of each modelling material.

   One mark should be awarded for suitable justification of each modelling material, e.g. modelling clay can be remoulded many times.

5. (a) (i) Note: environment here could mean either its working environment or its effect on the environment as a whole.
       Description of environmental issues could include:
       • Weather factors affecting its operation
       • Properties of materials factors, corrosion etc
       • Carbon footprint
       • Awareness of potential fire risk to the local environment
       • Ease of cleaning
       • Ease of maintenance
       • **Any other reasonable response.**

   Any two described environmental issues for one mark each.

       (ii) *Description of safety issues could include:*
       • Safety of user
       • Stability
       • Safety to local environment
       • Properties of materials relating to safety, heat, etc
       • Hot surfaces
       • Use of gas
       • **Any other reasonable response.**

   Any two described safety issues for one mark each.

(b) *Explanation should consider the following issues:*
- Identifying a need that is not being addressed by mainstream providers
- Narrowly defined group of potential customers
- Demand for a product that is not satisfactorily being met
- Small in comparison to the mainstream marketplace
- Specialization on small identifiable market areas
- **Any other reasonable response**

Any two explained issues for one mark each.

6. (a) • Primary functions versus secondary functions
- Pocket tool — scissors and various functions. Original tools had one function — multi-tool has several
- One main function plus additional uses or features

Two marks will be awarded for a described, clear answer.

(b) User trial, user trip, observation, user questionnaire

No marks for naming the technique, only for the description.

Two marks will be awarded for a described, clear answer.

(c) Shape of handles, curved lines, contrast in colours, logo stylish, plastic versus stainless steel, wow factor

Two marks will be awarded for a described, clear answer.

(d) Justified reason for stainless steel in context of this product strength/hardness/durability

One justified reason for one mark.

(e) Dip coat, powder coat, electro plating, spray painting

Two methods for one mark each.

7. (a) Morphological analysis, design stories

One mark per correct response up to a total of two marks

(b) **Design Stories:** to generate ideas using design stories you would put yourself in the place of the product you are designing. You would write a short story about a day in the life of the product or a story about the product being used. This then gives you a few ideas about what the product might need to do. This helps write the specification, which will lead to a range of ideas.

NATIONAL 5 DESIGN AND MANUFACTURE 2014

SECTION 1

1. (a) (i) *Any one from:*
- cherry
- mahogany
- teak
- walnut
- oak
- **Any other suitable response**

(ii) *A description that covers two of the following:*
- More variety of colours
- Aesthetic ('looks good')
- Durability
- Better quality
- Environmental
- Strong
- **Any other suitable response**

(b) *Any two from:*
- lap
- corner rebate
- mitre
- dovetail
- butt
- dowel
- biscuit joint
- **Any other suitable response**

(c) (i) *A description that covers two of the following benefits:*
- Improves the appearance of the wood
- Offers protection to the wood from bumps and scratches
- Gives a waterproof surface
- Gives a surface that can be easily wiped clean
- Makes the wood more durable/hardwearing
- **Any other suitable response**

(ii) *A description that includes two of the following points:*
- Remove pencil marks with eraser/sandpaper
- Sand wood smooth
- Dampen the wood to raise the grain
- Sand wood again with smooth sand/glass/garnet/wet and dry paper
- Steel wool (wirewool)
- Remove dust/use white spirit/damp cloth
- **Any other suitable response**

(d) (i) *Explanations indicating that:*
- Rounded corners prevent tearing of the plastic when it is being formed around the pattern

(ii) *Explanations indicating that:*
- Sloping sides allow the plastic to be removed easily from the pattern

(iii) *Any two from:*
- A plastic that has plastic memory/can be reformed if mistakes are made
- Can be recycled
- Available in a range of colours
- Can easily be vacuum formed
- Easy to clean
- Cheap
- Easy to work with
- **Any other suitable response**

(e) (i) *A description that includes two of the following stages:*
- Fit the tool
- Fit the piece of work in the chuck
- Adjust compound slide to 45 degrees
- Move compound/cross slide to create chamfer
- **Any other suitable response**

(ii) *A description that includes two of the following:*
- Fit the cutting tool
- Fit the piece of work in the chuck
- Move tool to the start of the cut with the cross slide
- Reduce diameter with either compound slide or apron wheel
- **Any other suitable response**

(iii) *Any two from:*
- Depending on the diameter of the material
- Depending on the type of material
- Depending on the process being carried out (knurling/finishing)

(f) (i) *Any two from:*
- It has a relatively low melting temperature
- Lightweight
- Does not corrode
- Does not require finish
- Aesthetic reasons ('looks good')
- Strong
- Durable
- Non-ferrous
- Easy to work with
- **Any other suitable response**

(ii) *Any three from:*
- Can achieve intricate detail
- Mass production
- Speed of production
- Inexpensive
- Surface finish/looks good
- Components are identical
- **Any other suitable response**

SECTION 2

2. (a) **Anthropometrics**
To gain marks, the relationship between the ergonomic consideration and the part of the bicycle must be described.
Areas that may be covered:
- Saddle length/width
- Distance from saddle to peddles/saddle to handlebars
- Distance between handles
- Length/diameter of handles
- Distance from handles to brakes
- Length of brakes
- Width/length of pedal
- Length of gear trigger
- Adjustable parts, eg saddle
- Different frame sizes
- Weight of cyclist
- **Any other suitable response**

Physiology
Areas that may be covered:
- Strength required to pedal/pull brakes/change handlebar or saddle height/turn handle bars & steer/change gear
- **Any other suitable response**

Psychology
Areas that may be covered:
- Overall look – reference to intended market/safety/ease of use
- Sound from gear change/brakes/steering
- Feel of grips on handle bars/brakes/saddle
- Gear number indicators
- **Any other suitable response**

(b) (i) *Example response:*
- Durability would be researched because the user would expect the bike to last for several years without breaking or weakening.
- The designer would need to research which materials and joining methods would be strong enough to resist knocks and bumps and be able to be used in all kinds of weather.
- **Any other suitable response**

(ii) *Example response:*
- Ease of maintenance would be researched because a bike would have to be regularly maintained by the user in order to keep it in good working condition.
- The designer may have to investigate methods of changing or pumping up tyres, oiling chains and cleaning so they could then make the bike as easy as possible to keep working safely.
- **Any other suitable response**

(iii) *Example response:*
- Aesthetics would have to be researched so that the design team would have a good understanding of what fashions and trends the intended market is interested in.
- A bike for young girls would have a totally different look to a bike for teenage boys.
- **Any other suitable response**

3. *Candidates may make reference to:*
- Reduction in packaging
- Miniaturisation
- Recyclability
- Upcycling
- Number of parts/ease of separation of parts
- Services offered by brand – removal & recycling of old
- Energy use in production/in use
- Energy use in transportation
- Materials
- **Any other suitable response**

4. (a) (i) Possible Graphic techniques:
- Rough sketches
- Annotated sketches
- Perspective sketches
- 2D sketches
- 3D sketches
- Sketches
- Roughs
- **Any other suitable response**

Example response:
A designer may use annotated sketches at the initial ideas stage because it is a quick technique, allowing them to sketch out various ideas and note their thoughts next to them.

(ii) Possible Graphic techniques:
- Working drawing
- Exploded views
- Assemblies
- Sections

- 3D solid CAD model
- Storyboard
- **Any other suitable response**

Example responses:
A working drawing would be used at the planning for manufacture stage as the design team would need to note down the accurate dimensions of the product.
The assembly drawing will help the team understand what it looks like and how the components fit together.

(b) Modelling Materials:
- Paper
- Card
- Corrugated card
- MDF
- Wire
- Pipe cleaners
- Foam
- Clay
- Modelling compound
- Balsa wood
- Expanded foam
- Sheet plastic
- Construction kit
- Wood
- **Any other suitable response**

Example responses:
Corrugated card is a good material for modelling as it can be easily joined with masking tape. (2 marks)
Designers use clay because it can be easily shaped with your hands and can be made into unusual shapes that can't be made with sheet material. (2 marks)

5. (a) (i) • Water/rust resistant
- Tasteless
- Aesthetics — modern look/matches other appliances
- Easy to clean
- Hygienic
- Resists chemical cleaners
- Ergonomic reasons
- Link to manufacturing process — available in sheet form
- Strong/hardwearing/robust
- Heavy (for stability during use)
- **Any other suitable response**

(ii) • Speed of production
- Economies of scale/cheaper
- Component accuracy
- Quality of finish
- Uniformity
- Reduced workforce
- **Any other suitable response**

(b) Injection moulding

(c) • Cost of equipment/machinery
- Cost to maintain equipment/machinery
- Cost of staff training
- Time for staff training/re-training
- Impact on environment of new equipment/ machinery
- Disposal of old equipment/machinery
- Can stay ahead of the competition/adapt designs/ new designs
- Allow new shapes/less joining techniques to be used
- Reduce unit cost

- Reduce labour costs
- Reduce material used
- Quicker production methods
- More accurate production methods
- Can facilitate rapid prototyping
- **Any other suitable response**

6. (a) *Example responses:*
Users could press the button to switch the razor on and off. They could then comment on ease of use. (2 marks)
The users could hold the razor and comment on how comfortable it is to hold. (2 marks)

(b) *Example responses:*
Comment on the shape of the razor.
Rate the colour of the razor on a scale of 1 to 10, 10 being the best.

(c) Possible answers:
- Eye-catching packaging
- Reduced or lower price point/introductory offer
- Promotional offers — BOGOF/free shaving gel
- Sell under a brand name
- Adapt to suit a new market segment
- Celebrity endorsement
- Specific advertising techniques
- **Any other suitable response**

Example responses:
A design team may decide to reduce the price of the razor when it enters onto the market. (1 mark)
A design team may get people interested in buying their products by offering an additional product, for example free shaving gel or moisturiser. (1 mark)

(d) Candidates must describe one of the following to gain full marks:
- Morphological analysis
- Brainstorming
- Technology transfer
- Analogy
- Lateral thinking
- Mood board
- Lifestyle board
- Take your pencil for a walk
- Design stories
- Gathering public opinion through a market survey
- **Any other suitable response**

Example answer:
Brainstorming
The team will sit together and note down all of the ideas each person has, no matter how silly they seem. Some ideas may spark off thoughts in others, allowing different suggestions to be explored in the hope of coming up with a new idea.

NATIONAL 5 DESIGN AND MANUFACTURE 2015

SECTION 1

1. (a) (i) *Statement of suitable equipment:*
- Held securely in a bench vice
- Quick release clamps
- 'F' clamps
- 'G' clamps
- Sash cramps/clamps
- Bag press
- Band clamp
- Hand clamp
- **Any other suitable response**

(ii) *A description that includes two of the following points:*
- The possible destruction of natural hardwoods (deforestation)
- Speed of growth (quick or slow)
- Pollution resulting from transporting hardwoods from tropical regions/less pollution from local sources
- Hardwood dust being produced during the shaping processes
- Hardwoods have a longer lifespan
- Sourced from sustainable forest/farmed hardwood forest
- Animals lose their home
- Hardwoods can be recycled
- **Any other suitable response**

(b) (i) *A description that includes two of the following stages with reference to the appropriate tools:*
- Measure/mark the centre line
- Measure/mark the four lines for holes
- Marking the hole centres
- Measure with a rule
- Mark with a scriber
- **Any other suitable response**

(ii) *A description that includes two of the following stages:*
- Secure metal/clamp metal/put metal in vice
- Cut small chamfer
- Guillotine corners off
- File surface into rounded shape
- Cross file
- Draw file
- De-burr
- **Any other suitable response**

(iii) *A description that includes two of the following stages:*
- Secure metal/clamp metal/put metal in vice
- Heat the metal to make it easier to bend
- Beat/bend with appropriate tool
- Jigs/former
- **Any other suitable response**

(iv) *A description that includes one of the following:*
- Use of a jig
- Use of a former
- Use of a template
- A bending machine/box folder
- Gabro set to angle
- Blanking and pressing
- A CNC bending machine
- Sand casting
- **Any other suitable response**

(v) *A description that includes two of the following stages:*
- Cross file
- Draw file
- Abrasive paper/block
- Remove grease/remove blue
- Apply a primer/base/under coat
- **Any other suitable response**

(c) (i) *State any two of the following:*
- Available as transparent/translucent
- Readily available
- Available in different colours
- Easy to bend or shape
- Easy to reform
- Easy to drill
- Easy to use
- Easy to cut
- Light weight
- Strong
- Durable
- No finish required
- **Any other suitable response**

(ii) *A description that includes two of the following stages:*
Heating stage:
- Heat the acrylic until it softens
Forming stage:
- Bend it around a former/jig
- Clamp and allow to cool
- **Any other suitable response**

(d) (i) *A description that includes three of the following stages:*
- Mark centre (diagonals) on one end
- Punch a hole in the centre
- Mark a line (diagonal) on other end
- Saw down the line
- Secure blank in vice
- Plane corners down/take corners off
- **Any other suitable response**

(ii) *A description that includes two of the following stages:*
- Remove/move tool rest
- Speed machine up
- Slow final cut/slow feed speed
- Use abrasive paper/sand it
- Use steel wool
- Use shavings (burnishing)
- Raise the grain
- Apply finish
- Sharpen the tool
- **Any other suitable response**

(e) *Describe any two of the following:*
- Increased use of bright colours
- Surface features such as stickers/decals/theme
- Added sound effect
- Add modern technology
- Moving parts
- Advertising
- **Any other suitable response**

(f) *A statement of a benefit to the environment:*
- Less raw material usage
- Less landfill use
- Less energy used to manufacture replacements
- Recyclable parts remain in use longer
- Animal habitat not affected
- **Any other suitable response**

SECTION 2

2. (a) (i) *Statement of suitable benefit:*
   - Available in large sheets/wide sheets
   - Readily available
   - Stable in varying temperatures/does not warp/twist/bow like timber
   - Cheap/inexpensive/tends to be less expensive than solid timber
   - Smooth surface/textured surface/flat surface/good surface for achieving a smooth finish
   - Strong/strong in both/all directions/cross grained
   - Hard wearing/durable
   - Uniform thickness/even textured
   - Light weight (in context of clock)
   - Easy to use (in context of clock)
   - **Any other suitable response**

   (ii) *Statement of suitable method:*
   - CNC router
   - CNC machining
   - Laser cutting
   - High pressure water jet cutting
   - **Any other suitable response**

   (iii) *A description that includes two of the following benefits:*
   - Quick
   - Identical products
   - Intricate detail
   - Smooth edges/good finish
   - Accurate
   - Shorter lead times
   - Cheap/inexpensive
   - Reduced labour costs
   - 24/7 production
   - Unskilled workforce
   - Nesting to reduce waste
   - **Any other suitable response**

   (b) *An explanation that includes two of the following issues:*
   - Manufacturer error leading to missing components/missing components
   - After sales customer care
   - Standard of raw material
   - Clear instructions
   - Some level of skill is required to assemble the kit
   - Having the correct tools to assemble
   - Guarantee
   - Quality of standard components
   - Checking the kit is not damaged in transit
   - **Any other suitable response**

3. (a) (i) *State any two of the following:*
   - Morphological analysis
   - Technology transfer
   - Analogy
   - Design stories
   - Lifestyle boards
   - Mood boards/mood rooms
   - Brainstorming/thought shower
   - Researching or looking at existing products
   - Lateral thinking
   - SAM(Subtract, Add, Manipulate)/SCAMPER
   - Take your pencil for a walk
   - Survey/questionnaire/market research
   - **Any other suitable response**

   (ii) A clear description of an idea generation activity attracts two marks.

   (b) (i) *State any one of the following graphic techniques:*
   - Sketches
   - Sectional views
   - Construction details
   - CAD
   - Orthographic/dimensioned drawing
   - Exploded views
   - **Any other suitable response**

   (ii) *State any one of the following graphic techniques:*
   - Presentation drawing
   - 3D solid model/CAD model/Inventor (any modelling package)
   - **Any other suitable response**

   (c) (i) *State any two of the following:*
   - To create/develop new ideas
   - To see it in 3D
   - To test design factors*
   - To show it to the client/other designers
   - To determine manufacturing/construction processes
   - To show a focus group to increase market share
   - Quick/easy to make
   - **Any other suitable response**

   (ii) *State any one of the following:*
   - Wood
   - Foam
   - Clay
   - Modelling compound
   - Balsa wood
   - Expanded foam
   - Polymorph
   - Polystyrene
   - Smart modelling material
   - **Any other suitable response**

4. (a) *Candidates should describe the following broad areas of aesthetics.*
   - Shape
   - Colour
   - Form
   - Texture
   - Material
   - Line
   - Proportion
   - Balance
   - Symmetry
   - Fashion/style/fad
   - Contrast
   - **Any other suitable response**

   (b) *A description that includes two of the following:*
   - Headband fits round head/ sized to fit human head
   - It is adjustable to fit a range of users' head sizes
   - Button sized correctly for finger
   - **Any other suitable response**

   (c) *Any two of the following statements:*
   - More flexibility for the user/increased mobility during use
   - Easier to tidy away or store
   - No tangle of wires to sort out
   - **Any other suitable response**

5. (a) *A description that refers to one of the following:*
- User trial/trip
- Testing
- Survey
- **Any other suitable response**

Any combination of the statements below would score two marks:
1. Hand out the product to a range of users
2. Carry out activity
3. Report back on results

(b) *A description that refers to one of the following:*
- Product comparison (this term scores one mark on its own)
- User trial/trip
- Survey
- **Any other suitable response**

For survey/questionnaire responses, any combination of the statements below would score two marks:
1. Hand out the product to a range of users
2. Carry out activity
3. Report back on results

(c) (i) *Write any one of the following:*
- The scooter should move easily over a variety of surfaces
- It should be easy to steer
- It must have a brake
- It must be stable whilst in use
- **Any other suitable response**

(ii) *Write any one of the following:*
- The scooter should be easily cleaned
- All parts should be easily accessed for maintenance
- **Any other suitable response**

(d) (i) *Describe one of the following:*
- Selects appropriate materials for manufacture
- Selects suitable joining methods/manufacturing techniques
- Selects a suitable finish
- **Any other suitable response**

(ii) *Describe one of the following:*
- Responsible for the project budget
- Manages purchases
- **Any other suitable response**

6. (a) *State any two of the following:*
- Purchase of machinery
- Associated computer hardware costs
- Manufacture of mould/tooling
- Training of workforce
- **Any other suitable response**

(b) *State any two of the following:*
- Injection point or mark
- Sprue mark
- Ejector pin marks/round indents where it has been pushed out the machine
- Tapered edges/draft angles
- Complex shapes
- Mould split lines/lines where the mould has joined or separated
- Shrinkage/sink marks
- Flash
- Webs
- Single part
- **Any other suitable response**

NATIONAL 5 DESIGN AND MANUFACTURE 2016

SECTION 1

1. (a) (i) Spinner made from low cost thermoplastic sheet.

One mark each for:
- Available in a wide range of colours
- Easy to form to the required shape
- Easy to work with
- Can be recycled
- Can be reformed if mistakes are made
- Hardwearing/durable
- Lightweight (to spin in wind)
- **Any other suitable response**

(ii) Forming thermoplastic strip.

A description that includes two of the following:
- Heat the thermoplastic until it softens
- Bend it around a former
- Leave to cool

(iii) Edge finishing.

Explanations indicating that:
- It is easier to smooth a flat edge rather than a twisted edge
- It is easier to hold/clamp the flat thermoplastic
- The thermoplastic is less likely to snap
- It is easier to access the edges
- **Any other suitable response**

(b) (i) Waste material.

Explanations indicating that:
- The gap allows space for the width of cut from the saw blade
- Inaccurate cuts will not damage the squares
- This would allow the edges to be finished to a square

(ii) Soft jaws.

Explanations indicating that:
- This avoids surface damage to the thermoplastic from the jaws of the engineer's vice

(c) Suitability of beech for top.

One mark for:
- It looks attractive
- It is easy to work with
- It is strong/robust
- It is locally sourced
- It is readily available
- It is durable/long lasting/hardwearing
- It can be sourced in an environmentally friendly manner
- **Any other suitable response**

(d) Sustainable forest.

Explanations indicating that:
- Managed forests where trees are replaced after harvesting
- When trees are cut down they are replanted
- **Any other suitable response**

(e) (i) Central hole marked out.

A description/graphic that includes the following:
- Draw the diagonals using a rule/straight edge

OR

- Measure half way along each edge with a rule
- Mark across with a try square and pencil

Option for marking centre:
- Indent the beech with a bradawl/scriber/centre punch
- **Any other suitable response**

(ii) Benefits of varnish.

A description that covers two of the following benefits:
- It enhances the look of the beech
- It protects the beech against moisture
- Extends lifespan
- Easy to clean
- Protects against physical damage such as bumps, scratches, scrapes, etc.
- **Any other suitable response**

(iii) High standard finish on beech.

A description that covers three of the following stages:
- Rub off pencil marks
- Abrade beech with rough abrasive paper
- Raise the grain
- Abrade beech with smooth abrasive paper
- Apply <u>layers</u> of varnish
- Rub down with steel wool
- Ensure the brush/cloth is not overloaded with stain
- Brush/wipe with the grain
- Brush/wipe out any drips or runs
- Remove any hairs that come off the brush
- Follow the instructions on the tin/spray can
- Spray from correct distance
- Build up thin coats as required
- **Any other suitable response**

(f) Reasons for brass.

One mark each for:
- Does not rust/corrode/weatherproof/non-ferrous
- Does not require a finish
- Easy to work with
- Strong/robust
- Durable/long lasting/hardwearing
- Acoustic qualities
- Aesthetic reasons ('looks good')
- **Any other suitable response**

(g) Manufacturing the chime.

A description that could include some of the following:
- Secure the brass in a vice
- Saw/cut the brass with a hacksaw
- File the rough edges left by the saw
- Use a flat file to angle the edge at a 45°
- Secure piece of brass in lathe
- Cut 45° angle (lathe tool)
- Create the flat end using a file
- Mark out the position of the hole using steel rule/ scriber/eng. square
- Centre punch the position of the hole
- Mount brass in machine vice
- Drill the hole with a pillar drill.
- Remove any burrs with abrasive paper/file
- **Any other suitable response**

SECTION 2

2.(a) A description of a suitable test to evaluate the function of the washing machine.

Test:
- In a laboratory the manufacturer would take a range of stained clothes and wash them. They would then examine the cleaned clothes and judge how well the machine performed

User Trial:
- Ask a range of users to clean a variety of dirty clothes over the period of a week and then provide feedback on how well the machine performed

(b) Environmental impact.

A description that covers any two of the following:
- Improve energy rating
- Energy use in production
- Eco friendly energy source
- Reduce volume of water used
- Materials
- Use recycled materials/recycle waste material
- Easily replaced parts
- Reduce packaging
- **Any other suitable response**

(c) (i) Suitable process for hinge.

One mark for:
- Die casting

(ii) Suitable material for hinge.

One mark for:
- Aluminium
- Zinc
- Stainless steel
- Brass
- **Any other suitable response**

(iii) Rapid prototyping hinge.

One mark for:
- See it in 3D (see what it looks like)
- Cheaper than traditional methods
- Quicker than traditional methods
- Changes can be easily made
- Problems can be identified at an early stage
- Alternative solutions can be made
- **Any other suitable response**

3. (a) (i) Wrist band ergonomics.

Candidates may refer to products similar to the wrist band.

Anthropometrics:
- The wrist diameter suits diameter of band
- Button size for finger tips

Physiology:
- The non-slip inner coating does not slide on the wrist
- Lightweight material

Psychology:
- The yellow numbers make you feel energised
- Makes a sound to alert the user
- **Any other suitable response**

(ii) Wrist band durability.

Candidates may refer to products similar to the wrist band.

Candidates may make reference to:
- Vibrations when exercising
- Withstand being dropped
- Weatherproof
- Sweat proof
- 24 hour a day use
- Scuffing
- Suitable material
- **Any other suitable response**

(iii) Wrist band aesthetics.

Candidates may refer to products similar to the wrist band.

Candidates may make reference to:
- Colour
- Shape
- Form
- Texture
- Line
- Proportion
- Symmetry
- Contrast
- Pattern
- Fashion
- **Any other suitable response**

(b) (i) Explanation of niche marketing may include:
- Targeting product at a very **specific** market
- Small but **focussed** market segment
- **Any other suitable response**

(ii) Explanation of market pull may include:
- Consumers need change resulting in new products being designed
- Other companies launch similar products to satisfy consumer demand
- **Any other suitable response**

(c) Suitable thermoplastic.

Material:
- Polypropylene
- ABS
- HDPE
- HIPS
- Nylon
- Polycarbonate
- **Any other suitable response**

Reason:
- Impact resistant
- Flexible
- Strong/hardwearing/robust
- Durable/long lasting
- Economic
- Easy to shape
- Easy to clean
- Wide range of colours
- Recyclability
- **Any other suitable response**

4. (a) Computer generated models.

Advantages may include:
- Can see/rotate in 3D
- Accuracy
- Produced quickly
- Long term economic benefit
- Easy to edit/change
- Can send/share electronically
- Ease of storage
- Easy to export to CAM/CNC/rapid prototyping
- **Any other suitable response**

(b) Standard components.

Benefits may include:
- Cheaper than producing yourself
- Speeds up production process
- Can be used on different products
- Reliable/quality assured by producer
- Ease of repair/maintenance
- Easy to source
- Will fit common tools
- Can transfer across different products
- **Any other suitable response**

(c) CAM.

Drawbacks:
- Setup costs
- Training costs
- Hardware/software costs
- Breakdown
- Deskilled workforce
- Employability issues
- Increased energy use
- **Any other suitable response**

(d) Brand name.

Benefits may include:
- Trust in a brand name/reputation
- Guaranteed sales
- Advertising
- Premium pricing
- Customer loyalty
- **Any other suitable response**

5. (a) Generate ideas from mood board.

Response must include aspects taken from the mood board.

Example
Look at the images on the mood board and use the colours/materials/patterns/shapes/etc. to influence/inspire your ideas.

(b) Open design brief.

Any of the following reasons:
- Can be more creative
- Gives them a wider range of research/ideas
- Diverse range of products for consumer
- Designer can have more influence/not client driven
- **Any other suitable response**

(c) (i) Initial ideas graphic technique and explanation.

Any of the following techniques with a suitable explanations:
- 2D/3D sketches
- 3D solid model/CAD model/inventor (any modelling package)
- **Any other suitable response**

Example
Initial ideas would be produced quickly using sketches.

(ii) Planning for manufacture graphic technique and explanation.

Any of the following techniques with a suitable explanation:
- Orthographic drawings
- Scaled up detail
- Exploded/assembly drawing
- 3D solid model/CAD model/inventor (any modelling package)
- Dimensioned views
- Working drawing
- **Any other suitable response**

Example
When planning for manufacture a working drawing must be produced. This will provide all the relevant dimensions clearly to the manufacturer, ready for production.

Acknowledgements

Permission has been sought from all relevant copyright holders and Hodder Gibson is grateful for the use of the following:

Photo of a BenQ computer mouse © BenQ Europe B.V. (Model Paper page 5);
Image © photoshaker-Fotolia (Model Paper page 7);
Photo of a Gerber multi-tool © Silva Ltd (Model Paper page 8);
Image © RAJ CREATIONZS/Shutterstock.com (2014 page 5);
Image © Cameron Spencer/Getty Images (2014 page 6);
Image © Quinn Rooney/Getty Images (2014 page 6);
Image © Bryn Lennon/Getty Images (2014 page 6);
Image © Dawes Cycles (2014 page 6);
Image © Alina Ku-Ku/Shutterstock.com (2014 page 8);
Image © rtguest/Shutterstock.com (2014 page 8);
Image © FEV/Shutterstock.com (2014 page 9);
Image © Wth/Shutterstock.com (2014 page 9);
Image © Gavran333/Shutterstock.com (2014 page 11);
Image © Africa Studio/Shutterstock.com (2014 page 11);
Image © Sandra van der Steen/Shutterstock.com (2014 page 12);
Image © Simon Krzic/Shutterstock.com (2014 page 12);
Image © Mehmet Dilsiz/Shutterstock.com (2014 page 13);
Image © Art Konovalov/Shutterstock.com (2014 page 14);
Image © Nixx Photography/Shutterstock.com (2014 page 14);
Image © Pakhnyushcha/Shutterstock.com (2014 page 14);
Photos of a model helicopter © Royal High School, designed by Gareth Sinclair (2015 pages 2–9);
Image © yampi/Shutterstock.com (2015 page 10);
Image © Nicole Gordine/Shutterstock.com (2015 page 12);
Image © Oleksandr Chub/Shutterstock.com (2015 page 14);
Image © Alexander Demyanenko/Shutterstock.com (2015 page 14);
Image © Alexander Kalina/Shutterstock.com (2015 page 14);
Image © Coprid/Shutterstock.com (2015 page 16);
Image © koya979/Shutterstock.com (2015 page 18);
Image © KKulikov/Shutterstock.com (2016 page 10);
Image © Budimir Jevtic/Shutterstock.com (2016 page 11);
Image © Chesky/Shutterstock.com (2016 page 12);
Image © YAKOBCHUK VASYL/Shutterstock.com (2016 page 14);
Image © Dmitry Morgan/Shutterstock.com (2016 page 14);
Image © TerryM/Shutterstock.com (2016 page 16);
Image © Yoko Design/Shutterstock.com (2016 page 16);
Image © AtthameeNi/Shutterstock.com (2016 page 16);
Image © james weston/Shutterstock.com (2016 page 16);
Image © James Steidl/Shutterstock.com (2016 page 16);
Image © meunierd/Shutterstock.com (2016 page 16).

Hodder Gibson would like to thank SQA for use of any past exam questions that may have been used in model papers, whether amended or in original form.